The Math of
NASCAR

Ian F. Mahaney

PowerKiDS press

New York

J
513
MAH

For Brenda

Published in 2012 by The Rosen Publishing Group, Inc.
29 East 21st Street, New York, NY 10010

First Edition

Editor: Joanne Randolph
Layout Design: Greg Tucker

Photo Credits: Cover Al Bello/Getty Images; p. 4 (left) David Walberg/Sports Illustrated/Getty Images; pp. 4–5, 6–7, 19 Shutterstock.com; pp. 5 (right), 12–13 John Harrelson/Getty Images for NASCAR; pp. 8–9 Andy Lyons/Getty Images; pp. 10–11 Ernie Masche-Pool/Getty Images for NASCAR; pp. 12 (inset), 14–15 Rusty Jarrett/Getty Images for NASCAR; pp. 16–17 Streeter Lecka/Getty Images; p. 18 Donald Miralle/Allsport/Getty Images; pp. 20–21 Fred Vulch/Sports Illustrated/Getty Images.

Library of Congress Cataloging-in-Publication Data

Mahaney, Ian F.
 The math of NASCAR / by Ian F. Mahaney. — 1st ed.
   p. cm. — (Sports math)
 Includes index.
 ISBN 978-1-4488-2555-4 (library binding) — ISBN 978-1-4488-2696-4 (pbk.) — ISBN 978-1-4488-2697-1 (6-pack)
 1. NASCAR (Association)—Juvenile literature. 2. Stock car racing—Mathematics—Juvenile literature. 3. Arithmetic—Juvenile literature. I. Title.
 GV1029.9.S74M29 2012
 796.720151—dc22
                                    2010028507
Manufactured in the United States of America

CPSIA Compliance Information: Batch #WW11PK: For Further Information contact Rosen Publishing, New York, New York at 1-800-237-9932

Contents

What Is NASCAR?

Have you heard of NASCAR? "NASCAR" is short for the "National Association for Stock Car Auto Racing." NASCAR is a sport in which men and women drive cars that are **modified** for racing. The cars' engines are more powerful than normal engines. Because the

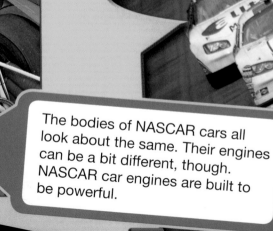

The bodies of NASCAR cars all look about the same. Their engines can be a bit different, though. NASCAR car engines are built to be powerful.

cars are going so fast, it can be a risky sport. The cars have many safety **features** to make the sport safer for drivers. The cars are also built to be **aerodynamic**.

The drivers compete against one another in races around the country. NASCAR has many fans of all ages. Math can help you learn more about this well-liked sport!

Figure It Out!

All cars have numbers. In this group of cars, which car has the middle number?

(See page 22 for the answers.)

NASCAR cars all have different sponsor names painted on them. A sponsor pays to put its name on a car. It costs about $8 million to be a main sponsor for a NASCAR car!

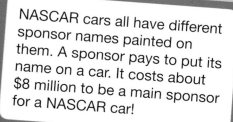

So Many Tracks

You might think that all NASCAR tracks are the same. It is true that most NASCAR tracks are oval. Not all ovals are shaped the same, though. This is true of NASCAR tracks as well.

Atlanta Motor Speedway
Atlanta, GA

Martinsville Speedway
Martinsville, VA

Infineon Raceway
Sonoma, CA

Pocono Raceway
Pocono, PA

It's a Fact!

NASCAR tracks have different shapes. Here you can see just a few of these shapes.

There are also road tracks in NASCAR. Road tracks are not ovals. They have many right and left turns in them. Drivers on road tracks often need to change how fast they are going to handle the turns.

NASCAR tracks are built in many different lengths, too. The shortest track is .5 mile (1 km) long. The longest is more than 4 miles (6 km) long.

Many fans come to watch NASCAR races. The largest tracks have seating for more than 100,000 people!

Figure It Out!

The Indianapolis Motor Speedway can seat the most fans of any NASCAR track. It has a **capacity** of 250,000. If the track sells 225,000 tickets for the Brickyard 400, how many empty seats will there be?

(See page 22 for the answers.)

About the Cars

The cars the drivers race in NASCAR are called stock cars. They are called stock cars because they look like normal cars that could be found in a car dealer's stock, or supply, of cars. The cars are much more powerful, though.

It's a Fact!

Cars are not the only NASCAR racers. Some NASCAR races are for trucks!

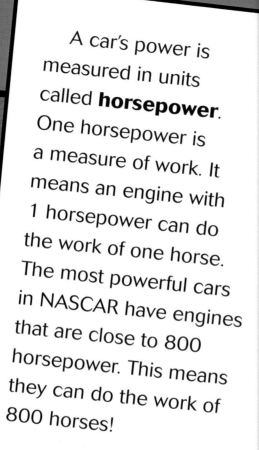

A car's power is measured in units called **horsepower**. One horsepower is a measure of work. It means an engine with 1 horsepower can do the work of one horse. The most powerful cars in NASCAR have engines that are close to 800 horsepower. This means they can do the work of 800 horses!

Dale Earnhardt Jr. drives a Chevy Impala stock car in a 2010 race here.

An engine in a normal car can be 200 horsepower. A NASCAR race car engine with 800 horsepower is much more powerful. How many times more powerful is an 800-horsepower engine than a 200-horsepower engine?

(See page 22 for the answers.)

Lots of Laps

The **distance** of NASCAR races is between 125 miles (201 km) and 600 miles (966 km). To drive these distances on a track, the drivers keep going around the track a certain number of times. One time around the track is one lap. To find the number of laps the drivers must make, divide the race length by the number of miles in one lap.

To help drivers and fans keep track of laps, a person waves different-colored flags to let drivers know what to do. A green flag like this one is waved at a race's start.

For example, a race called the Carfax 400 is a 400-mile (644 km) race. The race is run at the Michigan International Speedway. That track is 2 miles (3 km) long. To find out the number of laps the drivers must make, you would write a math **equation** like this one:

400 miles ÷ 2 miles = 200 laps.

Figure It Out!

You can use math to find out how many laps are left in a race, too. A NASCAR race is 150 laps long, and the lead driver has finished 96 laps. How many laps does the lead driver have to go before he finishes the race?

(See page 22 for the answers.)

Who Is the Fastest?

The faster a person moves, the farther she goes in a given amount of time. The fastest NASCAR driver will get to the finish line in less time than the other drivers. Of course, a driver's **speed** changes during the race. The driver who is the fastest at any given time changes, too.

Here Dale Earnhardt Jr. cheers after winning a 2010 racing series at the Daytona International Speedway, in Florida.

You could look for the **average** speeds of the drivers to find out which one is going fastest overall. Say a driver was moving at 195 miles per hour for one lap, 197 for another, and 199 for the last lap. To find the average, first add the three speeds. Then divide by the number of numbers in the group:

$$(195 + 197 + 199) \div 3 = 197.$$

Figure It Out!

The top five cars in a race are listed below. Their average speed in miles per hour is next to the car number. Can you reorder the cars to show how they will finish, from first place to fifth place?

Car #	Average Speed
16	195
21	194
25	191
26	192
42	197

(See page 22 for the answers.)

Kyle Busch is shown winning a race in July 2010 in Chicago.

Pit Stop Math

In NASCAR races, the drivers try to go as fast as they can. The drivers also need to make **pit stops**. During pit stops, each driver has a pit crew that changes tires and adds gas to the car. The pit crew tries to get the driver back on the track as fast as possible. The best pit crews can change four tires and add gas to a car in as few as 12 seconds!

Only seven people can work on a car during a pit stop. There are two tire carriers, two tire changers, one jack man, one gas man, and one person who catches spilled gas.

Figure It Out!

Car 25 leads the race by 2 seconds. Car 6 is in second place. Both cars stop in the pits at the same time to change their tires and refuel. Car 25 takes 16 seconds in the pits. Car 6 takes a 13-second pit stop. Which car leaves the pits in first place?

(See page 22 for the answers.)

The difference between an 18-second pit stop and a 12-second pit stop saves the car 6 seconds. Those extra seconds may make the car a winner!

Race Strategies

Each NASCAR driver and his crew have a **strategy** at the beginning of a race. They plan when to make pit stops. They may plan to make the first pit stop after 50 laps then the next one after another 50 laps.

If a tire blows out, the driver can lose control of the car. This can cause accidents.

Car 34 uses 1 gallon (4 l) of gas every two laps and it has a 22-gallon (83 l) gas tank. Can the car make its first pit stop after 50 laps? If not, at which lap will the car need to stop in the pits?

(See page 22 for the answers.)

Late in a race, a team may decide to keep the same tires on the car during a pit stop. This is called short pitting. It is done to save time in a close race. It takes less time only to refuel, and the car will get back on the track faster. It can be risky, though. Tires that are too worn will blow out. It is hard to finish a race first with flat tires!

The Chase

Each year, NASCAR has 36 races. During the first 26 races, points are given to drivers for winning races, the number of laps spent in the lead of races, and finishing well. In most races, first place is worth 185 points.

After 26 races, the 12 drivers with the most points qualify for the Chase. The Chase is the

Amazing Stats

Dale Earnhardt, shown here, won seven championships. He is listed as one of NASCAR's 50 greatest drivers.

name for the last 10 races of the season. In the Chase, those 12 drivers start with 5,000 points each. The driver who wins the most points during the Chase is the NASCAR champion.

Figure It Out!

In the Chase, drivers are given extra points if they win 1 of the first 26 races. Drivers receive 10 points per win. If a driver qualifies for the Chase and wins 5 of the first 26 races, how many points does the driver have at the start of the Chase?

(See page 22 for the answers.)

Jimmie Johnson won the 17th race of the 2010 racing season, shown here. This was his fifth win of the season. Each win gave him extra points going into the Chase.

Driver Stats

Have you ever heard people talk about a driver's stats before? "Stats" is short for "**statistics**." Many sports fans use statistics to help them know how their team or driver measures up to others in a sport. The most important stat in NASCAR is the standings or points totals. It shows who is in first place.

Jimmie Johnson won the points total and was the NASCAR champion in 2009.

There are other useful statistics, too. The average running position shows the average position in which a driver races during races. In 2009, the average running position of Jimmie Johnson was 8.660. This means that Jimmie Johnson could often be found near ninth place in a race. This running position was the best in NASCAR in 2009!

If a driver races the first lap in second place, the second lap in third place, and the third lap in first place, what is that driver's average running position?
A) 2 + 3 + 1 = 6.000
B) (2 + 3 + 1) x 3 = 18.000
C) (2 + 3 + 1) ÷ 3 = 2.000

(See page 22 for the answers.)

Figure It Out: The Answers

Page 5: Car 20 has the middle number.

Page 7: There are $250,000 - 225,000 = 25,000$ empty seats.

Page 9: A NASCAR engine is 800 horsepower $\div$ 200 horsepower = 4 times as powerful as the normal car engine.

Page 11: The lead driver has $150 - 96 = 54$ laps to go.

Page 13: If the cars are reordered by average speed, the finishers, from first to fifth, are:

Place	Car #	Average Speed
1	42	197
2	16	195
3	21	194
4	26	192
5	25	191

Page 15: Car 25 has a 2-second lead into the pits, which we can take away from its pit time: $16 - 2 = 14$ seconds. Car 6 takes 13 seconds in the pits, and Car 25 takes 14 seconds: $14 - 13 = 1$.
Car 6 leaves the pits with a 1-second lead.

Page 17: No, the car cannot wait until lap 50 to stop. Car 4 will have enough gas for $2 \times 22 = 44$ laps.

Page 19: The driver has 5,050 points going into the Chase:
$5,000 + (5 \times 10) = 5,000 + 50 = 5,050$ points;
or $5,000 + 10 + 10 + 10 + 10 + 10 = 5,050$ points.

Page 21: C) $(2 + 3 + 1) \div 3 = 2.000$

Glossary

aerodynamic (er-oh-dy-NA-mik) Made to move through the air easily.

average (A-vrij) A middle value of a group of numbers. It is found by adding the numbers and then dividing the sum by the number of numbers in the group.

capacity (kuh-PA-sih-tee) The total amount that someone or something can make or hold.

distance (DIS-tens) The length between two points.

equation (ih-KWAY-zhun) A math statement that says that two different things are equal.

features (FEE-churz) The special look or form of a person or an object.

horsepower (HORS-pow-er) The way an engine's power is measured.

modified (MAH-dih-fyd) Changed for a new purpose.

pit stops (PIT STOPS) Times when a car visits a place on the side of a racetrack to get gas and new tires.

speed (SPEED) How quickly something moves.

statistics (stuh-TIS-tiks) The study and understanding of groups of numbers.

strategy (STRA-tuh-jee) A plan to win the race.

Index

Web Sites

Due to the changing nature of Internet links, PowerKids Press has developed an online list of Web sites related to the subject of this book. This site is updated regularly. Please use this link to access the list:
www.powerkidslinks.com/sm/nascar/